this book is dedicated to:

the amazing, lovely, kind & wild

Because my heart grows new wings in your presence

With Love:

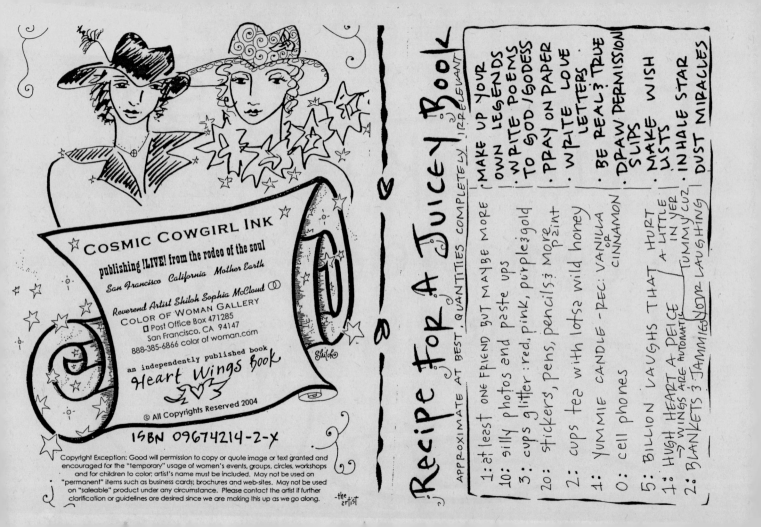

IDEA: Braid her hair and put tiny white blossoms in it and kiss her part...

This Little Book About Real Friendship was created with the same things that Make A Relationship Really Juicey......

abandon ✤ desire ❂ risk ♡ love ✤ pleasure ♡
willingness ❂ wonder ? faith ⚘
Joy ♡ Acknowledgement ✦ Trust ✤
forgiveness ♦ sweetness ♡ honor ✚
longing ❂ mystery ⚘ exploration ⇌ and therapy
and Questions ?!?

This little book has bits and pieces from many real friends and also make believe ones. Sometimes I want to have a slumber party and stay up all night with a friend I haven't even met yet. Sometimes we have to make it up or, better yet, learn to be a friend to your own sweet self.

Have you ever missed someone you haven't even met yet?

you can also give this to your own sweet self! ♡

sisterhood ♡
you are so many sweetnesses to me...

Me ♡ You

with melted butter ⊙ sharing everything ⊙ never being embarrassed ⊙ kissing your soft cheek ⊙ dreaming really big ☆ buying the same shoes ♡ Juicey Secrets ☆ pink Lemonade & champagne ♡ rose petal red ⊙ job soothing ♡ crying until we laugh ☆ finding carrots ⊙ swiss huge grins ⊙ watching old movies ⊙ collecting shells, bones & stones at the beach ☆ sitting too long with the car radio ⊙ pretending kitty and princess ⊙ dancing in the moonlight ⊙ painting our toe nails with purple glitter ♡ going to the cafe ♡ flirting @ getting the same tattoos ♡ talking about our life when we were mermaids ☆ chocolate at one time ⊙ reading poetry to each other ☆ cinnamon rolls ⊙ eating too much ⊙ knowing each other's favorite food ⊙ loving who we are...... ⊙ praying together

OH YA, I ALMOST FORGOT, OUR GUARDIAN ANGELS ARE BEST FRIENDS TOO...

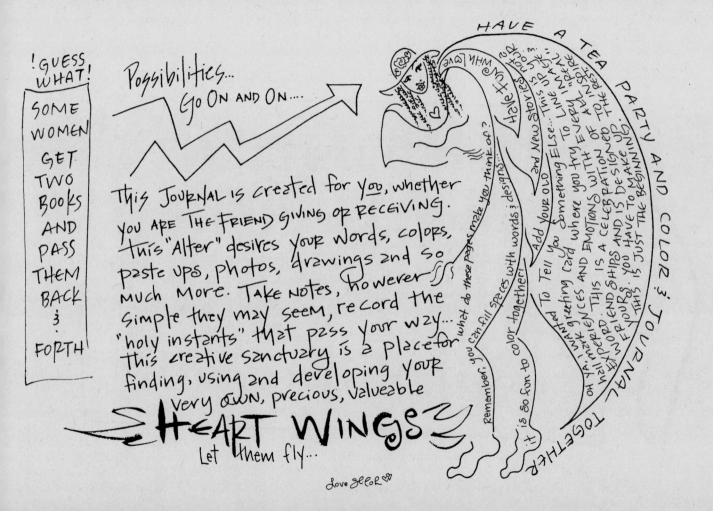

What is REAL?

"What is Real?" asked the rabbit one day. "does it mean having things that buzz inside you and a stick out handle?"

"Real isn't how you are made," said the Skin Horse. "It's a thing that happens to you. When a child loves you for a LONG, LONG TIME, not just to play with, but REALLY loves you, then you become Real. It doesn't happen all at once. You Become. It takes a long time. Generally, by the time you are Real, most of your hair has been loved off, and your eyes drop out and you get loose in the joints and very shabby. But those things don't matter at all, because once you are Real you can't be ugly, except to people who don't understand."

THE VELVETEEN RABBIT
By Margery Williams

I've been waiting to tell you how much it means to be gotten by you...

ANGEL FRIEND O' MINE

RESOLUTIONS

- ★ MAKE MORE MONEY (yeah...)
- ★ EXERCISE (yuck!)
- ★ CLEAN CLOSETS & GIVE STUFF AWAY
- ★ ~~STOP DRINKING COFFEE~~
- ★ READ LITERATURE & SELF HELP BOOKS
- ★ WRITE MORE LETTERS
- ★ LEARN TO USE INTERNET
- ★ START LOVING ME MORE
- ★ TAKE MORE BATHS
- ★ START DANCING WITH MORE ABANDON...
- EAT ICE CREAM & SHOP AS NEEDED

WHEN I MADE MY RESOLUTIONS LIST, YOU TOLD ME TO ADD "EAT ICE CREAM" AND "SHOP AS NEEDED"!

You told me I was feeling sorry for myself too much? Then you told me to get it together. So I did.

you called me when I didn't want to talk and made me laugh!

WHEN I
DON'T FEEL
LIKE
MYSELF
YOU ALWAYS
REMIND
ME THAT WHO I AM
IS CONTINUALLY CHANGING
AND THAT YOU LIKE
ME NO MATTER WHO I THINK I AM.

When I say I'm "fat"
   you tell me I'm juicey

When I tell you I am
"screwed up" you tell
me I'm mysterious

When I feel "hopeless"
you pray with me

When I am "done" crying
you take me shopping

When I didn't have a date for the company party, you showed up with roses, we were the best looking couple there!

WHEN I TOLD YOU TO LEAVE ME ALONE YOU WOULDN'T LISTEN — THAT WAS THE ONLY TIME I DIDN'T WANT YOU TO LISTEN — I SAID FOR YOU TO STOP LOVING ME AND YOU PUT OUT YOUR HAND. THAT IS WHEN I CRIED.

"NO MATTER WHAT ROAD I WENT RUNNING AFTER — YOU REMINDED ME THAT 'I CAN DO IT!'"

THE JOURNEY →

GO GIRRRL!

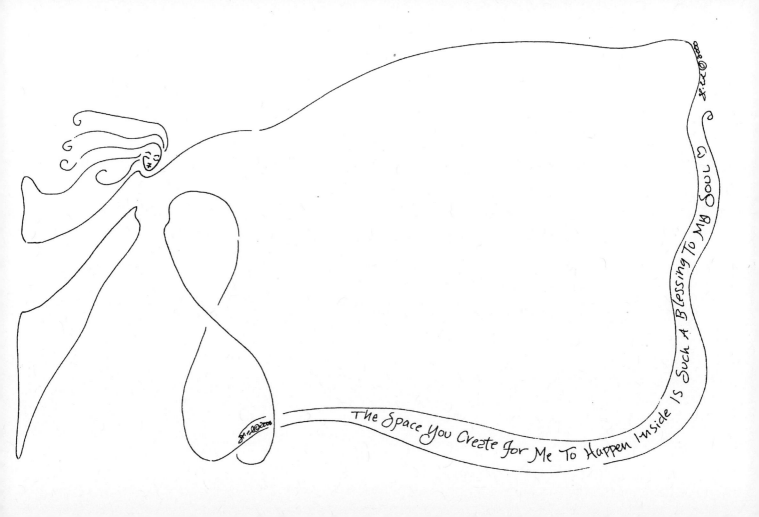

Remember that night when I drank so much red wine that I threw up on your shirt and asked you to marry me because you told me you didn't mind so much about the shirt...?

Sometimes you are so good and wise and beautiful I imagine I'm you — but then I miss myself, and I miss you even more...

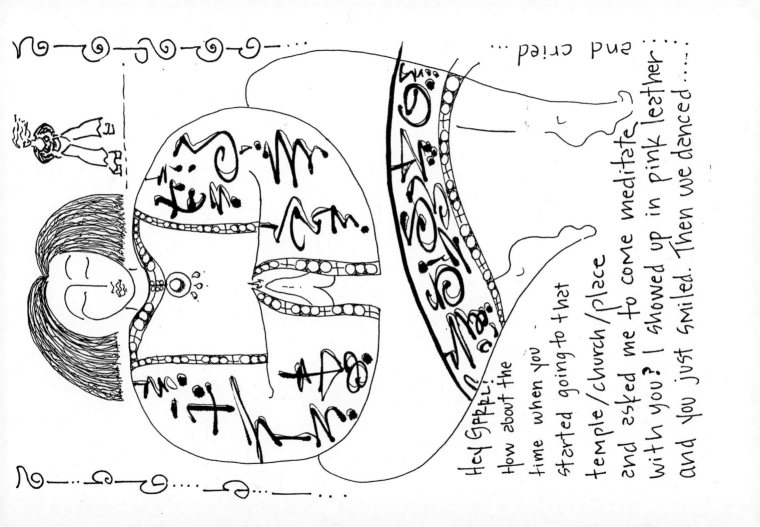

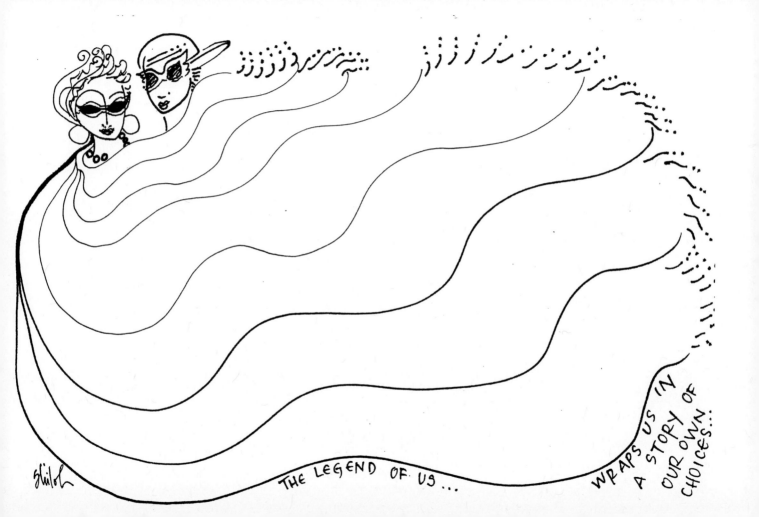

when they ask me why you are the friend for me... I will tell them: "because Her Heart was So Big... that she made my own heart grow huge just looking at Her!"

In the Presence of *Real Love* ♡ our Heart sprouts a set of the most gorgeous & powerful wings. Together we fly through our struggles and victories, soaring ever higher; past the comfort zone and up to OUR UNKNOWN Destinations...

...See you there!

NEW BOOK! SHE DANCES BETWEEN THE WORLDS!

Color of Woman

COLORING BOOK & JOURNALS by SHILOH MCCLOUD

"Our search for the divine feminine begins in our own lives. Color of Woman Journals will escort you to the deep places within you. She will be found there."
- Patricia Lynn Reilly, Author: *A God Who Looks Like Me, Be Full of Yourself!* and *Imagine a Woman*.

"A wonderful creative sanctuary designed to inspire a spiritual journey. Filled with 30 beautiful images, each of which holds the image of woman as Creator. 120 thick pages, so almost any medium can be used. A space to play, dream, heal, pray and create. I was so excited I wanted to jump right in and color!" - Feminist Bookstore News

"Shiloh's inspirational workbooks offer me a personal commitment. Coloring and writing in Color of Woman Journals creates opportunities to feel who I am and who I can become." - Charmaine Mandell, Author: *Remember Tomorrow*

"Shiloh's journals are an invitation to conscious life. I've had mine over a year and I discover that I pick it up when I want to explore with words and color all that is most essential to me as a woman. It's almost full and is a treasure trove of dreams, the lost feathers of gulls, petals of flowers, notes from my beloved friends, and secrets of the heart I would write nowhere else. Shiloh creates these journals out of her heart's love and her mind's joy. What a gift she's given us!" Christin Lore Weber, Author *Altar Music, WomanChrist, Blessings, Circle of Mysteries* and *Finding Stone*.

Color of Woman Coloring Book & Journal - 5th Edition Release - A Creative Sanctuary
In which to explore yourself through words, colors, shapes, textures and brushstrokes. You are invited to unlock the sacred chambers of your intimate thoughts, visions and mysteries. You are invited to a journey. Archetypal female images illustrated with strength, power, love and action. Color her braids, write poetry in her wings and witness yourself within herstory. 9X11

She Moves To Her Own Rhythm - Interactive Coloring Book & Journal - New Release - Guided exploration into the
spirit, body and soul of women. Images are accompanied by inspirational supporting text. Color, write and create in the flowing hair of the dancer, the tail of the mermaid, and the boots of the big mama. Ask yourself questions - what is the song of your soul? what did you really want to say? what will it take? when and how will you begin? Use this journal as a tool for exploring your wild woman, and your wondering woman. 9X11

Heart Wings - A Book About REAL Friendship - A Coloring Book & Journal - Brand New!
A celebration of the joys and trials that happen between two women who love each other. Filled with illustrations and quotes between friends as we splash in the sea, drink our lattes, go out dancing, protect each other, cuddle, dream and love each other for who we really are. This is a book for any and all friends, including one of the best friends of all, yourself! 9X5.5 NOTE: You can also have a set of greeting cards with these images ♡

30 ILLUSTRATIONS - 90 BLANK PAGES 110 LB. Thick Creamy CARD STOCK. Juicy Details: one inch thick, wrap around full color cover with spine and gilding text. You can use watercolor, pastel, acrylic & colored pencil.

we love women women women women

For more information or to order a creativity journal please contact your local bookstore or call 888-335-6866. You can also look us up at colorofwoman.com Thank you for your interest!

YOU ALWAYS REMIND ME ABOUT THE TRUE THINGS....

Thank you
For
Being
With
Me ♡

this is
Only
The Beginning...

I'm Shiloh and thank you for looking at this book. Everything I do is a work in progress, including everything I am. This makes life one big adventure with plenty of room for ~~mistakes~~ shifts happening. I believe that we cannot, must not wait for our "stuff" to be perfected before we acknowledge it and offer it up to "the great unfolding" as my cuzin' calls it. Creativity is a free gift given to each soul by the Creator in whose image we are created. We need to exercise our creativity and get REAL with the power it holds for all aspects of our life. Especially relationships.

YOU ARE THE ONE I HAVE BEEN LOOKING FOR ALL MY LIFE ♥

To Learn More About Shiloh's Creativity JOURNALS LOOK US By: COLOROFWOMAN.COM
888·385·6866

BLESS YOU ✛

OTHER JOURNALS INCLUDE: COLOR OF WOMAN & SHE MOVES TO HER OWN RHYTHM AND SHE DANCES BETWEEN THE WORLDS

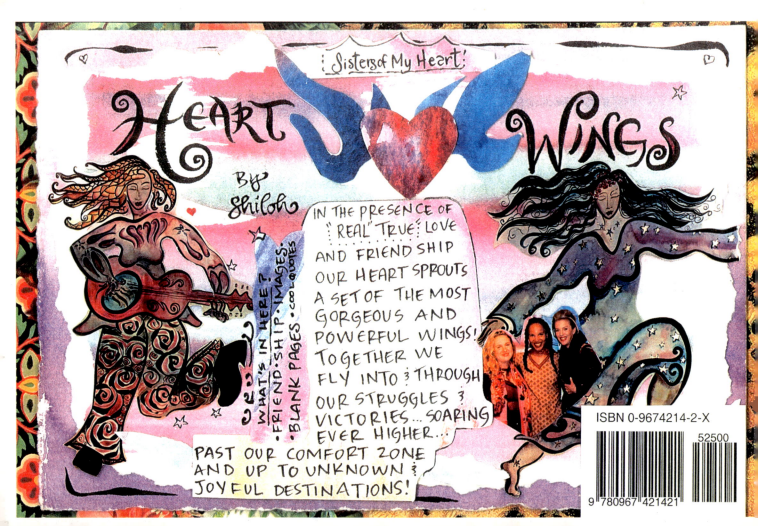